MW01180917

FARM STORIES | A Fading Dream

Loretta A. Johnson

Printed in the United States of America
First printing, 2017
ISBN: 978-1-54391-793-2

Books by Loretta Johnson
18712 5th Place S.W.
Normandy Park, WA 98166

Printed and Distributed by Bookbaby. Pennsauken, NJ

Cover design by Tori Day, DAYdesign
Edits by Denice McLaughlin

*These memories were written
by Loretta (Nepil) Johnson,
also known as Grandma Johnson
especially for Gabriel Kitsos,
Beatrice Kitsos, and Chloe Kambatta
in the year of 2017.*

I have so many memories
that I've collected through the years -
dreams and thoughts and feelings
and favorite family times.

I share them with you as a legacy
of love, and a personal connection
with my past.

·1·

A DREAM OF FARMING
1875-1914

This book was inspired by Chloe Khambatta, who when she would spend the night wanted me to tell her a story. I started telling her farm stories, even though I was not sure she would enjoy them. She loved hearing them, sometimes over and over again. In fact, she would go home and tell them to her mother. Denise, our daughter, would say, "Wow, I have never heard that story before!"

The book FARM STORIES | A Fading Dream, is based on my memories from 1947 - 1968, my Mother's diaries from 1940 – 1986, numerous life histories, excerpts from Big Sandy's weekly newspaper, *The Mountaineer*, and from LIFE magazine dated the week of January 27, 1947.

I am considered Full-Blooded Czech, as all four grandparents emigrated from Czechoslovakia in the early 20th century. There was an unconfirmed rumor that Grandma Nepil was twenty-five percent German. No one wanted to admit that after the war. Today, in a global world, it is not a factor.

My Grandfather, Frank Nepil, was born in 1887 in Cernovice, Czechoslovakia, where his Father, Anton, was the mayor. My Grandmother, Anna Michalek (or Michaela), was also born in 1887, in Steken, Czechoslovakia. In 1991, I traveled with my parents and daughter, Lorraine, to Steken and visited Anna's home. Steken is a very small market town about 60 miles from Prague as the crow flies. In the Czech language, the word Nepil consists of two words: NE = negatives "NO" and PIL + preterite of the verb "to drink". NEPIL can be translated into English as "no-drank". (I drank so I broke the first rule).

Frank and Anna both were teenagers in 1904 when for two weeks, they traveled on a ship from Czechoslovakia. Both grandparents arrived in Chicago at age 17, where they met and then married in 1907. Frank attended carpentry trade school in Vienna, Austria, and became a cabinet maker at the famous Art Institute in Chicago. They lived in Chicago, except for a short time in Wisconsin. After the Free Homestead Act was enacted, people rushed to stake out their claim and fulfill their dream of farming. Numerous Czech families headed for Montana. In 1913, the Nepil family joined the group with their three young children.

Jacob Sevcik, my maternal Grandfather, was born in Zelechovic, Moravia on July 25, 1875. My Grandmother, Emilie Sevcik was born in Zdare, (close to Brno) Moravia, a region of Czechoslovakia, on February 25, 1880. They had the same last name but were not related. They were married October 7, 1900. In 1906, Grandpa came to America alone, where he was employed as a baker, while Grandma and four children followed him to Chicago in 1907. Sadly, A two-year-old daughter, Emilie, died of whooping cough, shortly after they arrived. Grandpa trained to be a baker, and was part of the Baker's Union. After two years, they bought their own bakery, where Grandpa baked Czech pastries such as kolache, cream puffs, strudel, breads, and cakes. Grandma ran the bakery. Jacob, Emily and their four children, with a dream to become farmers, joined other Czech families headed for Montana in 1914.

· 2 ·

HOW IT ALL STARTED
1917-1946

D id you ever wonder how old I was when I had my first kiss, how I could drive without a driver's license, or why I was part of the group called Truancy Triplets?

Let's begin with the story of a boy named Laddie. He was the middle child of seven children born to Frank and Anna Nepil. Their homestead was located 25 miles southeast of Big Sandy, Montana. Frank left his artistry behind to pursue the adventure of becoming a farmer. They grew wheat on what eventually became 500 acres.

My Daddy, who was named Laddie, was born May 3, 1917 at home. A neighbor, who happened to be a midwife came to assist with the birth. Laddie, when he turned six, attended Hopp School. At that time, there were 28 kids from first to eighth grade, all in a one-room schoolhouse. Times were tough growing up for Laddie; he remembers many winters eating only rye bread and drinking coffee, nothing else. This was not a good diet for a growing boy! He and his brother made all of their toys; trucks, tractors and wagons. When he was five years old, his Mother had to go to Chicago to work at a factory as a seamstress. Sending home all of the money she earned was imperative to the family's survival. When his Mother was at the factory, his Dad traveled to Big Sandy to get supplies. One day, Laddie and his older brother and sister, (missing their Mother so much) took off walking to see her. They had no idea how far away she was. At nightfall, their Dad finally found them, after they had walked for eight miles! He and his siblings somehow survived a wandering stroll.

Finally, at eight years old, Laddie had his first planned trip to Big Sandy. His Dad took him to a silent movie. He fell asleep as he could not read the words fast enough. Big Sandy was a bit overwhelming, but inspiring, and he vowed to study harder to keep up with the silent movies, next chance.

In 1935 Laddie continued his adventures at Haugan, Montana, where he worked in the CCC (Civilian Conservation Corp) started by President F. D. Roosevelt. The CCC was instituted as a way to help with unemployment. They built roads, planted trees, strung telephone lines, and improved state and national parks by building campsites and trails. Daddy made only $30 a month, of which he sent $25 home. Laddie eventually followed in his Dad's career steps but in the reverse order, farming then building.

CCC buildings are covered with snow in 1936.

Meanwhile, Helen Sevcik (Laddie's soon to be wife) was born on January 15, 1923 on a farm just ten miles away from his farm, and 13 miles north of the Missouri River. She was the youngest of six children born to Jacob and Emilie Sevcik. Similar to Laddie's parents, Helen's parents were unable to resist the opportunity to settle the West, even with no farm experience. They had no electricity, telephones or gravel roads; yet her love of people, (thinking no fault of others), made her feel rich. The Sevciks were very proud of their Czech heritage. At nine years of age Helen started to help move cattle, and by 12 years old, she was riding alone in the Missouri River Breaks moving the cattle to water every day.

Unfortunately, her Father had to sell these cattle, due to the Dust Bowl and grasshopper plague! They luckily managed to survive on the small amount of money that they had saved. The hopefulness of free land was constantly coming up against the reality of having little money to live.

Now to the story of Laddie and Helen who started as dance partners at the country dance, and soon became life partners on January 17, 1942. This partnership would last 56 years. It was built on a foundation of love, kindness and caring, and out of it blossomed five children.

Helen and Laddie were married in Havre, Montana on January 17, 1942 by the Justice of the Peace. They were remarried at the Tent City Chapel in Kentucky on July 15, 1942. The witnesses at that time were their friends, Mrs. Walton and her nephew Leonard Biard.

Jerry Nepil, Edna Sevcik, Emilie Sevcik, Jacob Sevcik and Frank Nepil attending Laddie and Helen's wedding in Havre.

One week after their wedding, Laddie received his draft notice and would soon have to report to the Army. He could have been excused from signing up for the Army because he was married, but he felt that was his duty, and never revealed to the draft board that he was married. Helen would be left in charge of their only assets, four cows. Unfortunately, their precious assets all got into grasshopper poison and soon died. Helen wrote in her diary, "It's difficult to write Laddie about the cows", because he had saved so long to buy them.

Helen joined Laddie in Kentucky after he finished Basic Training, and they learned that soon they would become parents. Once again, life was proving to be very transitory, and in January, he was transferred from Ft. Knox to Camp Campbell, so Helen said goodbye again. Emily, Laddie's sister, invited Helen to come live with them in Chicago.

Their first child Marjorie, (my eldest sister) was born in Chicago on May 9, 1943. Sadly, Laddie was not able to be there with Helen for the birth of Marj, but Helen was proving to be a very strong and independent woman.

Laddie and Helen made for a happy young couple.

Helen playing in Chicago with Emily's dog.

Now, to tell you the story of Helen; her independence surfaced (even as a five and one-half year-old child) when alone she rode her horse Dolly, two miles to her one-room schoolhouse called Iliad. Either the older students or her teacher would take her off the horse in the morning, and put her back on in the evening. Many times, her horse got untethered and went home, leaving her to walk the two miles home alone!

Helen's Mother Riding Dolly in 1934.

Even though Helen had a determined spirit, raising a family was still daunting; Laddie was making only $133.59 a month as Staff Sergeant. In 2017, the average monthly wage was $3,679. Laddie had received a promotion and was transferred to Fort Smith, Arkansas. When they learned a second child was to be born in just 13 months, they felt financially unprepared. Carol Anne, the second born daughter, came into the world on June 25, 1944. They would share an apartment with other neighbors, saving money on groceries and rent. Barely able to afford groceries, the family needed a car, so they bought a 1939 Chevrolet for $800. Driving was limited however, because of the war and gas rations. Rubber was scarce, and thus, tires were not readily available, frustrating for

Helen who kept getting flat tires. Factories were busy making supplies and equipment for the war, so no one could buy a washing machine. Helen found a wash-board for 50 cents and did all of the laundry by hand. It was not until the war was finally over that she was able to afford a wringer washing machine.

As World War II was still raging in 1944, Laddie knew he would soon be sent overseas to help. In October of 1944, when it was time for Laddie to ship out to Europe, Laddie drove Helen and their two young babies back home (35 miles southeast of Big Sandy) to live with her parents. Laddie went back to Fort Smith, Arkansas, but didn't leave for France until January 28, 1945. There he became part of the 16th Armored Division in Germany under General George Patton. His division liberated Pilsen, Czechoslovakia which was the German's last stand in April 1945. General George Patton became famous and his life was featured in a movie in 1970.

Laddie in his Army uniform.

One of Laddie's love letters to Helen, Marj, and Carol Anne while he was still in Czechoslovakia reads:

> *I think I was right in or near the town my Mother was born in. I hear her say many a time where she was born but I don't remember the name of the place to the best of my knowledge it was near Pilsen. I would have never dreamt I would ever see this country but I guess the most unexpected things happen.*
>
> *How did VE day news strike the nation? Here it was just another day. That is, I didn't see any celebrating of any kind. I guess the reason for it was that there was resistance in Prague, for a couple of days after the war officially ended.*
>
> *Sweetheart, it is getting late so will close. With loads of love and kisses to my three girls.*
>
> *Yours forever,*
> *Laddie*

The war was officially over May 8, 1945 but Laddie had to stay in France until September.

· 3 ·

A LOOK BACK TO THE YEAR I WAS BORN
1947

Feeling grateful to be free of the war, Helen, Laddie and the two daughters move 24 miles southeast of Big Sandy, Montana near his family to take up farming. February 1, 1947, a Saturday, Laddie and Helen's third daughter Loretta Aileen was born, named after Loretta Gliege and Ailene McLeary, their friends from army days. I was born at 3:55 pm at the hospital in Havre, Montana; Mommy wrote in her diary that I was a happy and very loving baby.

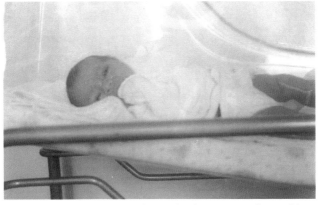

I was born 7 lbs 12 ½ oz. and 20 inches long. My Mother could not keep my sisters, Marj and Carol Anne, away from my crib. They wanted to wake me up and kiss me from morning until night. They cried when she would send them away.

In 1947 life expectancy was 62.9 years. I am happy to be writing this at age 70, while Helen, my strong spirited Mother, is still alive at 94.

Just as Loretta Aileen Nepil is born, Harry Truman is the President of the United States. The President, Franklin Roosevelt, had died in April 1945, and Vice President Truman succeeded to the Presidency. The Constitution had not yet been amended to allow for a new Vice President to be named, so the position remained vacant until the 1948 election.

The broadcast of the first soap opera, "A Woman to Remember," debuted in February. "Meet the Press" made its Network TV debut on NBC. None of this made any difference to us because we did not get TV until 1956. On occasion, we went to a neighbor's house to watch black and white television; however, they had such poor reception that we could hardly see anything!

Karo Syrup was an important ingredient for canning and freezing fruit. Dole pineapple was used for pineapple juleps, summer salads and pineapple party sundaes. Eggs sold for 23 cents per dozen but we had chickens that supplied them for free! Today, they sell for any price between $1.99 a dozen to $6.99 a dozen, depending on if you want them to be organic, vegan, vegetable fed, cage-free or free-range. Ours were always free range as we never bothered to build a fence! I don't recall losing any to coyotes (coyootes as we called them in Montana), weasels or raccoons. Although at night, the chickens were protected in the chicken coop. Vitamin D milk was 78 cents per gallon. Today, we pay $6.49 a gallon for organic milk. We milked our own cows twice a day, followed by pouring the milk into the large separator, which separated the milk from the cream. Our cows provided our milk, cream, and eventually fresh churned butter or ice cream. Fresh baked bread sold for 13 cents per loaf, today we pay up to $6.99 a loaf. White bread was the craze, but we enjoyed Mommy's fresh homemade rye bread, especially when it was warm from the oven! She baked rye bread weekly for 70 years. Bacon sold for 48 cents per pound, but again, we just butchered our pigs for our bacon. Today, many things are made with bacon, or bacon flavoring. Everything from bacon-flavored donuts to bacon-flavored ice cream have become the rage. Bacon is $6.43 per pound today. We were very self-sufficient, because in the summer our large garden, and fruit trees from western Montana, provided ample food for canning. Mommy canned peaches, cherries, green beans, sweet peas, tomatoes, and pickles. We would see steam from the large pans of peaches and cherries bubbling on the stove, and the glass preserving jars and lids jiggling in their baths of boiling water. It was necessary that she put up as much preserved fruits and vegetables as she could, providing food to last the winter. (I have often said that I grew up eating organic, local and sustainable, but I just didn't know it!) There was one health exception, that was that we would take the bacon fat, and render it until it became pork rind, a crunchy form of Cheetos. No wonder I have high cholesterol today!

Despite all the natural food, LIFE magazine started promoting every food that came in a can, "Food authorities agree – you can trust foods in cans." Promotions went on to say "Meals Mere Men Can Make; you can even turn a husband loose in the kitchen and expect a feast!" Of course, they never did, Mom did all the cooking. Today, it is trending for fathers to do most of the cooking in households.

In 1947, there were no credit cards. The grocery stores would let you sign your name (to charge it) and they would trust you to pay at the end of the month.

Famous movie stars and musicians born in 1947 included David Bowie, Billy Crystal, Elton John, Richard Dreyfuss, Arnold Schwarzenegger, Steven Spielberg and David Letterman. Songs made famous that year included White Christmas by Bing Crosby and Chi-Baba Chi-Baba by Perry Como.

In 1947, Mommy and other women usually only wore house dresses, slacks were only for picnics. There were no jeans for women. The "New Fashion Look" featured full skirts, V-necks and spiked shoes. When dressing up they needed to wear girdles that flattened the belly, and garter belts to hold up their nylon stockings. The nylon stockings had seams in the back which were difficult to keep in a straight line. Life magazine also started marketing candy with the slogan that "Crave for Candy" was a call for energy! No wonder they needed a girdle.

·4·

EARLY CHILDHOOD MEMORIES
OF FARM LIFE
1947-1956

My sister Carol Anne, and me sitting with our beautiful smiling Mommy. I was too camera shy to look at the camera.

I am having a fun time sitting up by myself on the lawn with Mommy and Carol Anne. Notice our car in the background.

Look how big I am, I can almost stand by myself!

My parents purchased 560 acres for $12.00 per acre in 1946, from Daddy's Father (Frank Nepil). In 1947, they paid $10.00 per acre to Choteau County for an additional 320 acres, (after the neighbors, Sturmas, had lost the property to the bank). Grandma and Grandpa Sevcik helped to finance this property, but in both cases my parents would pay interest to their parents. They taught us at an early age to pay your bills, and don't take advantage of your parent's financial help. Later, the house (on Sturmas land) got struck by lightning and burnt to the ground.

Sturmas standing in front of their house.

My parents, Laddie and Helen Nepil, bought a house from a neighbor, Lester Rutledge, and moved it to Uncle Jerry's land (Frank and Anna's farm). Eventually, after painting and wall papering, they moved the house to our farm; it took numerous neighbors, and a bulldozer, to move it. There was not a professional mover involved, neighbors helped neighbors.

House moving day.

The house had a large living room, a combination kitchen/dining room, and one bedroom. The three girls slept on a sofa bed in the living room. We did not have a bathroom, as we did not have running water, toilet or tub, thus, the outside toilet came into the picture. In the summer, it was great to disappear to the outhouse, in the winter months, not so much so. We looked at the Sears & Roebuck or Montgomery Wards (known as Monkey Wards) catalogs; you may wonder why the catalogs, but you see that was our source of toilet paper. We felt fortunate when Mommy would buy peaches, as they would come wrapped in soft tissue paper.

In 1948, Marj is five years old and holding me, the one-year old. Carol Anne is four years old; we all are sitting on a piece of cement that served as the front step.

Water was also a special commodity. We caught the rain water in a barrel (today environmentalists refer to that as harvesting rain water), and only bathed at home on Saturday night, so that we were clean for church on Sunday. There was no hot running water, so we heated the water on the stove and poured it into a wash tub, (in which we hardly fit). We never needed hair conditioner, as the rain water was quite soft. Water for drinking, and cooking, would be hauled from the "crick" (Montana's pronunciation) or creek, stored in the cistern, and then heated. The cistern was built below ground as a cement chamber, to store and preserve our water supply. We used the red hand pump to fill the buckets then carried them into the kitchen.

We did not get electricity installed until 1949. I laugh, because without lights, it was easier to get us to bed on time. For many years, if we had a lightning storm, I would be very frightened until Daddy would get the house grounded. In the 40's and early 50's there was not a national electrical code requiring a separate ground circuit, like there is today. I felt safe from the lightning after he hooked the power line to the ground circuit. We were all very saddened when Morris Flannery, a neighbor, fell to the ground when installing our electricity. He became wheelchair bound for many years.

That same year, we had the telephone line strung on the fence, the telephone was a wood wall-hung telephone with a hand crank that rang the bells. Our number was three long cranks and one short one. It was a party line, with 12 or more neighbors on one line, and very easy for the neighbors to "rubber in" and hear your news. A series of clicks on the line told you that the telephone operator, (and one or two neighbors) were listening.

It was so exciting, (for the whole family) when in February of 1952, the addition to the house was finished. Plumbing was installed. We then had a separate kitchen, additional bedroom, and, an indoor bathroom with real toilet paper.

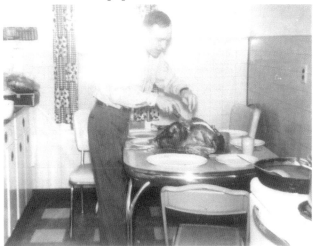

Daddy is carving the turkey in our new kitchen. This would be the window used in our drive-in restaurant.

Daddy had also managed to build us a playhouse under the stairs. It had a door on it so we could play house with dolls for hours. Our entertainment was quite simple, (with no TV and few toys).

They didn't trust me with a balloon!

We had a radio so my parents would listen to Paul Harvey and the news. This is where we would hear the famous closing line, "And now you know the rest of the story." He captured what we felt when he said, "We were poor, but we didn't know it." In those days, I don't remember ever being hungry, there were no government bureaus to determine where poorness begins and ends. We also listened to the Lone Ranger and Tonto (the duo conquering evil), there they would often call each other 'Kemosabe', which meant faithful friend. We had a small record player for entertainment but we only had one record, so we quickly memorized the words to "Blueberry Hill" by Fats Domino! If we got bored listening to our one record or the radio programs, we would play Cowboys and Indians. Of course, my sisters would be the Cowboys, that left me as the Indian; they then proceeded to tie my feet together and my hands together. I tried walking like that, and fell on my nose, after that Mommy made them quit. Our black and white television came when we moved to Big Sandy in 1956. I have never been a big television fan, but did get hooked on watching soap operas in college. My favorite, *Days of Our Lives*, started on November 8, 1965, and I never missed a show. Our family did not own a color television until January 28, 1968.

Marj, Carol Anne and I all became card sharks at an early age, the three of us girls played canasta and pinochle with our parents. The whole family went to card parties at the one-room schoolhouse, I was barely six years old, but confidently scooted right up to the table. When Frank Drga Sr, a 55-year old man, would say, "Who is my partner?", I would step right up and say "I am, and I am lucky at cards." When we won, he would later say, "Yes, I have to say you ARE lucky!"

In the summertime, our fun included swimming in the Eagle Creek on Osterman's land. It was a creek (or crick) and not very deep, but there was one water hole that allowed us to get completely wet. Although, it was a challenge to stay away from the leaches and swim.

Marj is six years old, Carol Anne is five and I am two and one-half. At only 25 ½ years of age, Mommy has three children. If we wanted to have any trees for our picnics, we had to travel to the Missouri River. My namesake Loretta Gliege is visiting us.

Our farm animals also kept us busy, the dairy cows were Nellie and Jersey (sometimes called Boss by Daddy). When I was seven, we got a cow from our neighbors, the Lidstones, we could not think of a name, so we named the cow Ethel after Mrs. Lidstone. We were told never to tell the Lidstone family what we had named the cow. One day we gave Bonnie Lidstone, their daughter, a ride to Big Sandy. I was sitting in the backseat, and said to Bonnie, "Guess what we named our cow!". My parents turned around immediately to give me a glare, but they were too late, as 'Ethel' had already come out of my mouth.

I am sitting in the back seat of our car.

It was a sad day when on Carol Anne's birthday, our Jersey cow (Boss) died of milk fever. It was up to us to feed her calf (named Carl) with a bottle, until he was grown. Once Carl got off the bottle, he did not pay much attention to us, so life went on.

We had a few beef cattle for butchering, but never got attached to them. It was very important that nothing was wasted, and that we learned the importance of sustainability. It was common that we ate liver, heart, tongue, and brains from the beef cattle. Mommy, also, would cook a roast beef, and then can it for winter food.

Carol, Mary & Loretta

Carol Anne is holding the bottle/bucket of milk, while Marj and I are hugging Carl.

Of course, there were dogs. The first one was called Buster. Buster got mean and tried to bite Marj. Mommy's diary says we had one called Blackie, but in my mind, he was called Puppy (another innovative name by the Nepil family). We probably called him Puppy until she thought of the name Blackie. We also watched a couple wild tom cats and wild rabbits, but we couldn't play with them. We would buy baby chicks, (sometimes as many as 150), they were kept warm in the Brooder House until they were old enough to be butchered. Sometimes, we lost one of them when they would squish each other in an attempt to keep warm. That was normal, often how the weaker chicks were weaned out. Some of the chickens would be spared to be laying hens, and it was our job to pick the eggs. Sometimes, we would have to lift the chicken up to get eggs, this was scary. But, we did have fun playing catch with the eggs on the way from the chicken coop to the house! Once we broke two, then we quickly ran to the house to have something left to put in the refrigerator.

We are standing in front of our truck with the chicken coop behind us. We hired Junior Webster to help harvest a couple summers. He liked to reach into the truck bed and grab some wheat to eat. Daddy would say, "he was eating all the profit." I think he was kidding, as we farmed 1000 acres of wheat and barley. Although, you let half of the fields rest each year, so there were only crops on 500 acres.

There were a couple of jobs that required a strong stomach, or a good place to hide away and avoid having to help with these chores. One was feeding the pigs. They were always muddy and their food would soon become slop. The other foul job was butchering the chickens. Daddy would set up a chopping block between the chicken coop and the garage. He would get his hatchet and quickly grab them by the feet to decapitate them. The decapitation was not as bad as the headless chickens squawking and flipping around the farm yard. The next step, plucking the feathers, was even worse. The bodies were scalded in a huge pot of boiling water, so the feathers would come off easily, but the pin feathers had to be burned or picked off. I helped with this task numerous times; cleaning of the chickens was not my expertise. I ruined one by puncturing some part that made it inedible, and was never asked to help again, (thank goodness)! It was not uncommon for my mother to butcher 30 chickens in a day. Helen's butchering activities often became news in The Big Sandy Mountaineer, our weekly newspaper. She sent frozen chickens and eggs to our relatives in Chicago. They all made the trip just fine.

Sometimes we visited the neighbors, or our cousins, and rode their horses. Daddy felt that horses were no longer necessary for our farm, and only created extra work for him. We had never had horses as pets, so didn't really know if we were missing anything.

Carol Anne and I are riding horses at the Martins' (our cousins) farmhouse in Livingston, Montana.

When it came to chores, I preferred outside, rather than inside. My sisters were always old enough to cook and wash the dishes. We did not get an automatic dishwasher until 1954! I was only allowed to dry the dishes, which got very boring, so I went out in the farm yard to help Daddy. I was the "boy" that he did not get until the fifth child came along. I was content to get his tools, or to hold something while he fixed it.

I (barely seen behind the rear mirror) thought I was "driving" the tractor and "pulling the drills". The drills were used to seed the wheat.

My nickname soon became "Jigger" (which came from a small glass that you would fill with a jigger of whiskey for your drink). I was also called "Chovaczech" which I believe meant small child. My favorite hobby was combing my Daddy's hair while he sat in his chair. He had a bald spot he claimed he got from wearing a helmet in the army, so there really wasn't much to comb. When Grandpa Sevcik came to live with us, I would spend hours combing his hair. His long natural curly white hair kept me occupied for longer.

Left to right: Uncle Chuck, Grandpa Sevcik, Grandma Sevcik, Carol Anne, Marj, Grandma Nepil with me, Mommy and Aunt Emily.

Though my Mother can speak and write Czech, we did not learn much of the language. The only words I can recall: Ano = Yes, Ne = No, Dobrow Noc = Good Night, Dobry' Den = Good Day or Hello, Jak Se Ma'te = How are you, Prosim = please and pivo = beer.

Celebrating that I am three years old, with my sisters (Marj at six years of age and Carol Anne at five) along with our two-year old neighbor Gerald Rutledge. Carol Ann is really laughing as she just stole the rocking horse.

Carol Anne at seven, Loretta at four and one-half, and Marjorie at eight posing for a professional photograph by Helmbrecht Photography. Our hair was curled with bobby pins, the only thing available!

A key part of living on a farm was that everyone had chores,and pitched in; responsibility was taught at a young age. During harvest Daddy would drive the combine, and Mommy would drive the truck, full-time, for at least two weeks; that meant my two oldest sisters and I would run the farm house. During the summer of 1951, we were running the house alone (Marj was eight, Carol Anne was seven, and I was four and one-half).

In the country, the substantial noontime meal was "dinner" and the evening meal was a cold "supper". While my parents were in the field all day, we made large meals (meat, potatoes, gravy, vegetable and salad), and would deliver dinner to them in the field. My job was mainly to sit in the back seat, and hold the lids on the pans. Marj would drive the car out to field, which could be a distance of five miles. Her only accident was when she pulled the auger home from the field. The auger tipped over in the ditch, but no one was hurt. A grain auger is used to move grain from the truck bed into the granary for storage, then later moved back to the truck when you decide to sell the wheat. Carol Anne learned how to bake pies and cakes at a very young age. Also every afternoon we would drive to the field with coffee and dessert, for my parents' mid-afternoon snack. The evening meal was light, and usually consisted of sandwiches, and maybe soup, prepared by Mommy and Daddy, allowing us to finally be off duty from cooking.

We were back on duty in the evening when Marj, at eight and I at four and one-half, would milk the cows. The milking was not an easy task, as the cows would swing their tails around batting at flies. Their tails often hit us in the head and caused us to lose focus. They would also take a step up, and nearly kick over the bucket of milk. The worst part was when the cow decided to take a poop, and you had to quickly grab the bucket and move it out of the way!

Grandma and Grandpa Nepil had moved from the farm to Great Falls in 1948. Sometimes, we got to visit them in the "big city" of

Great Falls. It was assumed by everyone, (except me), that Grandpa Nepil was a good barber. He, literally, put a large bowl on my head, and cut the hair around it. That was a traumatic day!

I am viewing the antelope with Grandpa Nepil while on a vacation. I have forgiven him as my bowl cut hairdo is starting to grow out.

We enjoyed living only 11 miles from our Grandma and Grampa Sevcik. At times, we would spend the night at their house. The house, which was built from mud blocks (adobe), and then painted white, consisted of two large rooms. The one room was the kitchen/dining/living room, and the other was the bedroom. They never did get running water or indoor plumbing. The coal burning stove was in the kitchen, so that would keep the room warm all night. The beds had big thick white quilts, but it was cold climbing into bed. I remember getting cold during the night; Grandma's solution was to put the hot water bottle in bed with us, and that made it quite toasty. She always had cinnamon-sugar pancakes rolled up in the cupboard, waiting for us. We also picked dandelions, and then helped make dandelion wine.

Grandpa and Grandma's house in 1925 and their Model T car.

In the summer of 1950, Mommy and her two brothers and two sisters were planning a 50th wedding anniversary party for their parents. After a month of being sick from a stroke, Grandma Sevcik died at the age of 70. She never wore her pretty turquoise dress, as she died a month before the party. Grandma Sevcik loved to take care of Marj, Carol Anne and myself, and we loved staying at her house, so she was dearly missed. After Grandma passed away, (and was buried in the Big Sandy Cemetery), Grandpa Sevcik moved to our farm and stayed with us for five years. Daddy had built a two-room apartment attached to the garage for him to live in, but Grandpa joined us for all his meals. This was a lot of extra work for Mommy and Daddy, especially when they had five kids to care for. Caring for elderly parents was a very loving, and common gesture in those days. That was the first time I got a good look at Grandpa's glass eye; evidently, he had a piece of coal fly up causing him to lose his eye.

We were very close with our neighbors, and established a tradition of getting together for Christmas, Thanksgiving and monthly dinners. There always was an aroma of mouthwatering gravies and sauces emanating from the kitchen. My favorites were the wonderfully fragrant apple pies, and thick chocolate frosted cakes, which seldom survived more than one meal.

My Mother later gave me her copy of *Woman's Home Companion Cook Book* which was published in 1953. Today, July 31, 2017, Chloe and I make our favorite Swedish Pancakes recipe from this cookbook.

SWEDISH PANCAKES
Flour, 1 ½ cups
Salt, 1 teaspoon
Sugar, 2 teaspoons
Eggs, well beaten, 3
Milk, 3 cups
Butter, melted, 3 tablespoons

Sift flour; add salt and sugar; sift again.
To beaten eggs add milk and melted butter; pour into flour mixture and stir until combined. Bake on hot greased griddle, using 1 tablespoon of batter for each or pour ½ cup batter onto griddle to make large pancakes.

The recipe calls for tart jelly and powdered sugar but we enjoy honey vanilla greek yogurt and fresh berries.

We had a large black upright piano with gargoyles on the side. It was in our bedroom, and at night I was terrified by those. We took piano lessons from Mrs. Giebel in Big Sandy, she was very strict, and would get upset if I did not cup my hands like I was holding an orange, or if I did not practice enough, in preparation for our recital. Needless to say, I did not become a famous pianist!

My clothes were usually hand-me-downs from Marj, and then Carol Anne, and would probably be saved for Lorraine. I remember my Mother making us three matching red and white dresses. She had an old Singer treadle that was powered mechanically by a foot pedal, her feet pushed it back and forth like a rocker.

In 1950, we finally got a wringer washing machine and got rid of the washboard. Mommy would take the machine outdoors and plug it in, using a long extension cord to an outlet in the garage. You had to take each piece of clothing and run it through the wringer, hoping that you would not get your arm caught. In good weather, you would take the clothes pins and hang each piece of clothing on the clothesline. During the winter months, Mommy would have a folding clothes rack indoors; we did not have an automatic dryer. In Big Sandy, she insisted on having a clothesline in the yard, as she liked the outdoor smell on the newly dried sheets. There were no dry cleaners in the area, so if we needed anything cleaned we would bring out the trusty wringer washer, and used gasoline to dry-clean the clothes. It was another challenge trying to keep the gasoline from catching on fire! We didn't seem to heed the warnings about the dangers of cleaning laundry with gasoline. The Reputable Dry-Cleaning Company concluded: "Even if she does her cleaning outdoors, there is still the greatest danger of all: the invisible menace of static electricity."

In August of 1952 my parents, two sisters and I, left behind the farm chores and took a vacation to Yellowstone National Park. This was the first time that we saw a bear! We three girls had gone up the cement stairs to the bathroom, when we came out we spotted the bear, and all started screaming. My legs could not keep up with running down the stairs, so I just rolled to the bottom. My parents wanted me to jump in the car (even though the bear was not coming near us), because they were concerned I may have been injured in the tumble.

In 1952, there was no way to determine the sex of the child before birth, so every time one of us was born the doctor and Daddy thought it was going to be a boy. When I was nearing my sixth birthday, my Mother was pregnant, and due to deliver on the 26th of December. One day my Mother came home from a checkup, and said, "The doctor said it sounds like a boy." I said quickly, "Tell doc – no way, we want a girl," (I was afraid a boy would wreck the

Christmas tree). Daddy stayed with us while Mommy was in the hospital. We loved his cooking, especially his square biscuits, he just didn't take the time to cut them out with a glass! Thankfully, Mommy gave birth to my sister Lorraine on December 26th, 1952, and we were able to keep the Christmas tree up a little longer!

Mommy had wanted two children and Daddy had wanted three children, so they had five. They had to try so many times in order to get a boy, so finally, on January 18th, 1955 Darell was born. We would play house and dress Darell like a girl, which didn't make Daddy very happy, but Darell would love all the attention from his sisters. As he got older, it was just as I predicted; he got under the Christmas tree and knocked it over many times, but he turned out to be a great brother.

When Mommy went to the hospital for the birth of Darell, our teacher Mrs. Diacon stayed with us. She was the worst cook, and all she made for breakfast was Cream of Wheat, I would nearly gag every morning. She made us stay at the table until we were finished, so if she looked away I was quick to find ways to hide her food in my napkin or hand. Whew! Oftentimes I would feel like an only child, as Marj and Carol Anne were only 13 months apart and Lorraine and Darell were only two years apart. I was happy for the differences in age, as I always felt it made me more independent and self-confident.

Christmas 1955, after Lorraine and Darell joined the family. Carol Anne is all set to start baking with her apron on!

In 1953, when Lorraine was two and I was eight the addition to the house was completed, and we became bed partners. I remember once she woke up in the middle of the night crying, "Daddy, Daddy, there is a chicken in my bed!" Daddy ran into our room in his shorts and t-shirt, then started feeling around in our sheets. Meanwhile I am trying to keep from laughing, as it was my long toenails that were mistaken for a chicken scratching her!

Back in the 50's and 60's you would curl your hair with rollers, then sleep on them all night. A very odd incident about me with rollers, is one Sunday morning I got up and I noticed that my hair was sticking out from the rollers. When we got back from church I went to make my bed, and found scraps of my hair. I also found more scraps of hair on the scissors that lay on the sewing machine stored in our room. I must have gotten up in the night and cut my hair without any recollection, then returned the scissors to the sewing machine (all the while lying next to Lorraine). Hmmm.

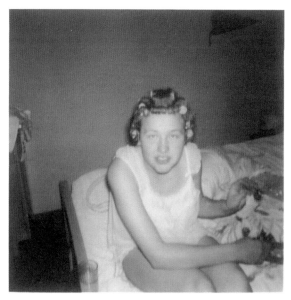

At age 15, I am a real fashion statement with my rollers.

· 5 ·

A ONE-ROOM SCHOOLHOUSE
1947-1956

A one-room schoolhouse was started when a home in the country was too far from the towns' school transportation. When country schools were formed they were managed by the parents. In those days one-room schoolhouses were very common in rural communities. There had been over 190,000 one-room schools in the early 1920's but only 28 operate in the United States today. Presidents Abraham Lincoln and Herbert Hoover attended one-room schoolhouses; perseverance, pranks, and pride abound in the words of those who attended one-room schools.

When Daddy attended Hopp School in 1923, there were 14 families managing the schools. While I attended, Hopp School usually consisted of about 10 to 12 students, and only six families. Daddy served on the School Board from 1950–1956; School Board members were responsible for interviewing and hiring the teachers. The parents provided cleaning, repair and maintenance on the school house, plus our mothers provided a hot lunch on Friday. It was difficult to get a teacher to come and teach in such a remote area. Teachers were challenged with teaching, and organizing a curriculum, for an average of 11 pupils ranging from grades one through eight. In addition, the teacher had to cope with a lack of running water and an outhouse that was across the school yard. The teacherage (where the teacher lived) was two rooms attached to the schoolhouse; one room was the kitchen/dining/living room, and the other room was the bedroom. There was a white pot with a lid (called a chamber pot) to use in the night; the rest of the time, she would use the same outhouse that we used. The schoolroom had one door, and the sides were built from wooden slats painted white, or shiplap as they called them. It had windows high up on the side, which kept the students from being distracted. Hopp and Illiad, another country school nearby, were in the same district. The Chouteau County Superintendent of Schools, Margaretha Thomas, would come several times a year to listen to us read, recite poetry, then ask us literature questions. Sometimes, we would perform skits or present musical performances for the parents. We also were required to travel to Fort Benton for achievement tests or Mommy loaded us, other students, and our desks into the truck, and took us to the Illiad schoolhouse for testing. My mother started both of my sisters in school when they were five years old, but they were lonesome so they officially waited until age six to start.

Marj, Gerald Rutledge (our neighbor), Mrs. Pearson (my sisters' teacher), the birthday girl, and Carol Anne are waiting to eat my birthday cake.

Students at Hopp School in 1950-51 include back row: Denny Osterman, Marj Nepil, Jack Flannery, Carol Osterman, front row: Faye Osterman and Carol Anne Nepil.

Standing left to right: Faye Osterman, Marj Nepil, Carol Osterman, Denny Osterman, Carol Anne Nepil and Jerri Ann Nepil (our cousin). In 1951 girls wore dresses with long white stockings to school every day.

I was anxious to start school at five since my sisters were there; I was fine not waiting until six. My first-grade teacher was Mrs. Donner, followed by Miss Holmes, and third and fourth grade teacher was Mrs. Diacon. Miss Holmes could barely climb up the front steps, we were sure that she had lied about her age; the mandatory age limit was 65. Usually, the teachers were single, but Mrs. Donner had two sons (Michael and Arthur) who attended Hopp School.

Once when my sisters and I were performing a musical for our parents, as third, fifth, and sixth graders, the crazy Mrs. Diacon insisted on putting Kleenex in the bust line of our matching red and white dresses! In her mind, she must have thought we were performing in Carnegie Hall.

In the rural classroom, getting the children to master basic literary skills came foremost to a teacher's mind. Regularly, we would have to spell, or read aloud, or write with strong emphasis on correct grammar. Practicing our penmanship was another important requirement. We always started the day with the Pledge of Allegiance to the huge American flag, standing together with our right hand over our heart. The room contained a work table with the globe of the world sitting on it, an old piano, and three rows of double wooden desks. There was enough room for the teacher to walk up and down the aisle, keeping an eye on what we were up to. We had reading, spelling, penmanship, and arithmetic in the morning. Lunch was followed by story time, health (physical education called P.E. today), and music or art. Science, history, and geography were added in the fourth grade. On Fridays, we had a weekly spelling bee, where we were called up one by one to the front of the class, spelling the words we had been learning. The Palmer Method of Penmanship (Cursive) was taught; today it is seldom used or seen; though still taught randomly in all but seven states. The younger grades worked on Manuscript or Block letters, while grades four and up worked on Cursive letters. The letters of the alphabet (both small and large) were posted above the blackboard. We all used fountain pens and ink bottles, when spilt the ink was deadly at leaving stains. Older students assisted the younger ones with common lessons.

We would often throw Kleenex spitballs at the blackboard when the teacher's back was turned. Our best prank was to sneak her yardstick and then scoot up and hide it behind the piano. At the end of the school year, when the parents were cleaning the school, they could not understand why there were so many yardsticks behind the piano. Another thing we did was to say we were sick at the same time that our friend said she was sick, fibbing so we could both be sent to the teacherage, rest on the teacher' bed and have a pillow fight.

The six students in the back, from left to right, are Carol Osterman, Faye Osterman, Carol Anne, Marj, Denny Osterman, and Jack Flannery. The future students, in the front, are Holly Osterman, Me, Glen Nepil, Blanche Nepil, Gerald Rutledge, Susan Merrill, and Jerri Ann Nepil. The desk that we used is on the right.

Joining us in this picture, were some of the parents. Mommy is taking the picture, and I am the third one on the left.

School was from 9:00 a.m. to 4:00 p.m. with an hour for lunch, and a 15-minute recess in the morning and afternoon. We had great fun playing games during lunch and recess. Some of the games were Tag, Anti-I-Over, Crack the Whip, Red Rover, and Mother May I. During the winter, I was happy to stay indoors and play house in the cloakroom with my boyfriend Michael Donner. We didn't have cloaks but the cloakroom was a small room where we put our coats and lunch boxes. We would play that he and I were husband and wife, and my classmate Susan was our child. We would save bits of our lunch so we could pretend that it was our dinner. Of course, the husband and wife had to kiss each other and now you know my first secret. Carol Anne and Marj were jealous, so they had to spoil it by telling my parents! Reluctantly, I had to quit.

On Friday, the parents would bring hot lunches which were a great treat after eating sandwiches all week. Ella Osterman made homemade donuts, so of course they were consumed rapidly. We would always have a special birthday party at school and usually had both a chocolate and a white cake.

I don't look very happy for my birthday party. I was a third grader and 7 years old at the time. Marj is holding Lorraine and Carol Anne is holding Ralph Merrill.

We would often walk to school; sometimes Daddy would walk with us if we had to cut through the field and the deep snow. There could be days with blizzards that would keep the roads and school closed. In 1954, the coldest temperature ever recorded, was in Montana, where it registered 70 below zero at Rogers Pass.

We are ready for school on another Montana winter day.

One year we had a very mild winter with little snow, so we rode bikes to school nearly every day. Of course, I had the hand-me-down bicycle, and one day after we had picked up our cousins it happened to break apart. One wheel rolled down into the ditch, and all of a sudden I was riding a unicycle, with no learned skills. Of course, my sisters and cousins laughed so hard they peed their pants. Jerri Ann had to stand on the register in the floor while her underwear dried, a common occurrence if you got wet from the snow, or didn't make it to the outhouse in time. After that, I finally got a new bike.

When I was in the third grade I had all my work done ahead of my classmate. Since the teacher was so busy with all the other grades, she could not take the time to get me started on my fourth-grade work. She suggested I simply get out of school one month early. Grammar was not my best subject, so all I had to do in order to be counted as present, was to write a letter and send it with my sisters. I especially loved going to stay with our neighbors, Leo and Elva Matchett, as I was Elva's 'special love', and it was boring at my house. She loved my blonde hair, green eyes, and that I liked to cuddle. They did not have any children at home, so I got lots of attention. My fourth-grade teacher also wanted me to skip a grade, but my parents did not approve. I was glad of this later, even at 17 I was the youngest in the high school graduating class, and if I had skipped, I would have been only 16 years old when I entered college.

Mrs. Diacon was probably breaking the law, since she brought her granddaughter to school with her for most of my fourth grade. Her granddaughter had hydrocephalus, (an accumulation of fluid on the brain) and needed a lot of care. It was Carol Anne's job to babysit her most days; I don't think the School Superintendent would have approved of that. We were guilty of harboring a secret!

In 1953 and 54, we belonged to Jr. Reserves, which was for children of farmers that belonged to Farmers Union. We would have regular meetings, summer camps, and even attend an occasional dance. During the school year dances were held at the Hopp School, while summer dances were held at Osterman's Grove (an old barn that had its roof blown off). These summer dances always started with a potluck picnic, then country dance music at dusk with songs coming from the accordion, piano and guitar. My sisters and I watched from the car until we fell asleep, then Daddy would carry us to bed at 2:00 a.m. They danced the night away, and on occasion, they danced until 4:00 a.m.

· 6 ·

EARLY CAREERS
WHILE LIVING IN THE COUNTRY
1947-1956

As I mentioned earlier, my sisters and I would run the farm house during harvest. They earned $3 a day and I earned $1 a day. We would want to drive as much as possible, and we always had permission to park the car in the shade of the house. It took a long time to find shade around the farmhouse, and while looking we came up with the idea that we could have a drive-in restaurant. Mind you, the In and Out Drive-in was opened in 1948, but McDonald's and Wendy's did not open until the 60's. We would take the screen off the kitchen window, and two people would be in the car while another one would be our waitress in the kitchen. We would order root beer floats (we made our own root beer), milkshakes, cookies, and cakes. This was all passed back and forth on a large cookie sheet.

The payment we received from my parents for running the farm house was used at our homemade "drive-in" restaurant. I received the least, because I was too young to do a lot of the cooking and baking. At some point I saved $10, and I decided I would spend it when we went into Big Sandy. I went to the grocery store and bought six jars of peaches and pears baby food. I also bought cucumbers and a couple of chocolate bars. I got my bag nicely in the car, and Mommy said, "Whose groceries did we get by mistake?" I said meekly, "Those are mine." She said, "Why would you buy cucumbers when we have them growing in the garden?" I was then told I needed to return my items. I was only five and very upset, but respected what I was told to do. After that, I spent my money on clothes!

When my sisters were 12 and 13, they made more money working for neighbors during harvest than at home. In August of 1956, Marj worked at Lannings for $4 a day, earning a total of $60 for the season. Carol Anne worked for Jenny Rutledge for the same wages. Carol Anne's job included weeding the garden early in the morning, washing windows, and butchering and cleaning many chickens. In August of 1959, I was 12 and worked for Muriel and Joe Silvan. I babysat their three young children, along with cooking all the meals, doing dishes, and cleaning house. The kids kept me very busy, and one time I caught them with matches below the front step. Thankfully, they did not burn the house down on my watch. By that time wages had increased, and I got $5 a day, where Carol Anne had moved up to $10 a day, ironing and baking for Mrs. Busta.

Even as bad as those jobs were, the job of picking rocks for Daddy was worse. I know it is hard to understand what is entailed with picking rock. When you plowed to plant wheat, it was necessary to remove all the medium to large rocks. Removing rocks prevented damage to the equipment, and allowed the wheat to fully grow. Sweat would run down our faces from the Montana heat, and wind was a constant blessing, with our dust filled bloodshot eyes. The only entertainment we had, (and one that we would fight over), was who got to move the truck forward 50 feet. I don't recall what our pay scale was but I know we did not earn union wages!

· 7 ·

TRAUMAS, ILLNESSES, AND ACCIDENTS
1947-1964

TRAUMAS

I was only three years old, when I accidentally saw our dog Buster get shot because he turned "mean" and tried to bite Marj. Our other dog Blackie got run over by a salesman as he was driving away from the house. It was still very sad even though it was an accident, since Blackie liked to chase cars, and bark furiously.

At age four, a very traumatic event made a real imprint on me. It happened on March 18, 1951, when Uncle Jerry and Aunt Ann's house burnt to the ground. I remember standing at the living room window crying, so afraid that something awful would happen to Daddy as they fought to save the house. Daddy stood on a ladder, fighting the fire with only a fire extinguisher. Mommy's diary indicates the house was destroyed within an hour. They saved very little as there wasn't much that people could do without a fire department.

The only good news was that my cousins were able to move to our farm, and stay in the two-bedroom apartment next to the garage.

Thus, we played a lot of games with Jerri Ann and Glen. It also meant that Grandpa Sevcik had to move into our house.

When Grandpa Sevcik and Grandma Nepil died, it was a very sad time for all of us. I was 10 years old that spring of 1957 when they died within two weeks of each other. Traditionally, Daddy never showed a great deal of emotion, except for that day. Daddy while holding my hand said, "Jigger, it's going to be okay, try not to cry." I then looked up and saw his eyes filled with tears.

The next trauma may not be traumatic for everyone, but it sure was for me even if I was 12 years old. This was the time the rat was hiding in the bottom drawer of the stove. Daddy and Darell were in the kitchen with the baseball bat trying to get the rat to come out. Lorraine and I were assigned to hold the glass screen door up against the door opening, so the rat wouldn't get into another room. Meanwhile, Mommy and Carol Anne were standing on the dining room table screaming. They managed to kill the rat only after hitting the glass in the door and breaking it into many small pieces, leaving a bloody mess. Now you know, it is a hereditary gene that all of the women of my family are afraid of mice and rats.

ILLNESSES

I was first hospitalized at less than a year old with double pneumonia, in November of 1947. A cousin had died of pneumonia so it was frightening for my parents that I had such a high fever, and it came on very quickly. If someone got sick it was an hour drive to the nearest hospital. The doctor's office was in Big Sandy, and even that was at least a 30-minute drive. It could be a harrowing trip on gravel roads that often were covered with mud, snow or ice. The doctors had quite a struggle to get my fever to come down; a new drug, Sulfa finally worked. I was in the hospital for nearly three weeks, and with no health insurance the bill was a prohibitive cost for my parents. For many months, my mother sold chickens to the hospital for $ .30 a pound, and eggs for $ .60 a dozen, helping pay

Dr. Aubin's $30 bill, the $52 hospital bill, and the $19 bill for prescriptions.

In 1954, the second hospitalization came the summer between second and third grade, I wasn't feeling well and had a high fever at the July 4th celebration. It was 95 degrees (as the high of the day), and a constant wind was blowing the cottonwoods. In Montana, the wind blew nearly every day; 124 mph the highest recorded to date. There was a large picnic and dance at Osterman's Grove. I waded in the creek and tried to cool off, but nothing would help my high fever; I finally got to bed at 2 a.m. when the dance was over. The next day I was raced to the hospital with strep throat, (today, they would not hospitalize you), but I was hospitalized for three days. If that was not enough, I was quarantined, and could not have any company. I couldn't even walk down the hall to meet the other kids. I felt so lonely. A very nice nurse would put her mask on, and come in and color with me, much to my relief. This event however never made an entry in my Mother's diary, so I must not have been too ill!

I was graduating from the 8th grade in May of 1960, and while I sat on the auditorium stage, I started running a fever. My brother was sick with the German measles, and I soon joined him. My parents had a long-planned trip to visit my Mother's sister, in Walla Walla, Washington. They were determined to take the trip. So, on the third day they just packed us up, measles and all, and took off. "We're going on vacation come heck or high water," they said. We had to have our food brought out to the car, while they ate in the restaurant.

In Spokane, we stopped to visit a former Big Sandy priest, and I was wearing my watch on the outside of my sweater, so the red spots would not creep out and expose measles. He said, "I have never seen anyone wear their watch like that." I said to myself, "Yes, and you have probably never seen anyone trying to cover up their measles!"

When I was entering high school in September 1960, I developed a terrible rash between my toes and fingers. This was especially embarrassing when you would clasp hands, dancing with a boyfriend. I was taken to the doctor in Big Sandy where it was diagnosed as athlete's foot (not sure what it was on my hands). After a treatment with Absorbine Jr. (that did not work), I was taken to Dr. Kendall in Great Falls, who said I was allergic to leather! We then ordered these very ugly moccasin-type shoes, (which I wore out the door and took off as soon as I got a block away). Thankfully a doctor in Missoula finally said, "Oh, use this cortisone and you will be cleared up in a week." Sure enough, he was right, and it was "goodbye moccasins" and the perfect medicine for my eczema.

February 1, 1964, my 17th birthday, was spent in the hospital for tests, due to the beginnings of an ulcer. I was in the hospital for three days and would only get a poached egg or Cream of Wheat cereal. This was for all three meals, all three days! I didn't like Cream of Wheat so by the ninth meal of poached egg, I was ready to throw it at them. I was beyond restless, and twisting the curtains so tightly they nearly came off the rod. The other people in for ulcer tests had been released that Monday morning. My mother begged the doctor, and I finally got released at 9:00 p.m.!

I thought I was too old to get the three-day measles in March of 1964, but that was not true. I looked in the mirror in the morning, fell back against the corner, and fainted. I finally got up and went out to the kitchen, and my parents asked, "Where have you been?" and I casually said, "Oh, I was passed out in the bathroom." They kept a closer eye on me after that!

ACCIDENTS

I had an accident in the fall of 1949, which could have been more serious than it was. We were returning from visiting Grandma Sevcik, I was sitting in the back seat, and even as a three-year old I decided that the door was not closed properly, and I needed to close it. This was before seat belts, so as soon as I opened the door it flew open, and I went with it. Carol Anne was sitting in the back with me and she screamed, "Mommy, stop! Loretta is dragging outside the car." I am not sure if it was better or worse, but I hung on to the handle the whole time. My Mother liked to speed, my guess is that she was going about 35 miles per hour, on a gravel road. Mommy came to a screeching halt and ran around the car to my door. By then I had lost my shoe, and had bleeding knees. I remember trying very hard to pretend I was a "big girl" and knew what I was doing. As soon as I knew that I was going to survive, the tears came quickly.

I survived my nearly tragic accident, and soon after, I got blamed for one of Carol Anne's accidents. In 1950, Daddy was digging a hole into which he would pour cement, and that would become our cistern. It was getting quite deep, and I wanted my sister to see how deep it was. She came running over to look, and at the same time a little dust storm came up and got dust in her eyes. This blinded her and she fell into the hole. She yelled at me, "Go get Daddy and Mommy," (thinking all the time that I might not do that). I surprised her and Daddy came out and got the ladder to go down and get her. To this day, she still considers it my fault that she fell in, as if I pushed her! She may be teasing me but it seems like a long time to hold on to something, especially when this accident had not been significant enough to make it into my Mother's diary.

The biggest accident happened in April of 1951, when I rode with Grandpa Sevcik to pick up my sisters and the Osterman kids from school. He was nearly 80 years old by then, and because of the glass eye, his sight was impaired. On our way home, he struggled with shifting uphill, and all of a sudden we started to roll backwards and to the right. Grandpa seemed to panic, and not know what to do. Thankfully Marj had learned where the emergency brake was and grabbed it. Ostermans, and other neighbors had to come and pull the car back on to the road. I was so upset when my doll fell down the deep ravine (we called it a coulee in Montana), and no one could get her out. From that day on, Grandpa Sevcik would never drive again.

My younger sister and brother had several accidents that required a hurried trip to the doctor in Big Sandy. In January of 1954, Lorraine had just turned two, she was running around the circle of the interior of our house, fell and cut her eyebrow on the sharp corner of the high baseboard. Two stitches later, she was as good as new, although she carries the scar still today.

Darell's accident was more serious, on August 14, 1956, as a toddler he had just gotten up from his nap, with a wet diaper. He decided in the middle of the day that he needed some light in the living room, and proceeded to try and plug in the lamp. Carol Anne was babysitting, Daddy was in town building our house, and Mommy was in Havre shopping, but Carol Anne quickly called and got ahold of neighbors who rushed him to the doctor. He was diagnosed with second-degree burns on his stomach and thumb. Farming neighbors knew it was essential, and sometimes life-saving, to help one another.

· 8 ·

FEARS ABOUT MOVING TO BIG SANDY
1956-1959

In 1957, my oldest sister, Marj, would start high school 25 miles from our farm in Big Sandy. My parents did not want to board her in town, so they decided that we needed to move. The school bus did eventually travel as far as our farm, but not until April of 1965.

Daddy, with the help of his brothers and Grandpa Nepil, would build us a new house in Big Sandy. It was a very nice three-bedroom home that was painted pink and white, (yes, in that day you would paint the top and bottom two different colors). It would later be turquoise and white.

We moved into Big Sandy on September 3, 1956 and I started the fifth grade. I would be leaving a school with 11 students, and going to a school that had 200-300 students, which made me very nervous. The elementary school would consist of Kindergarten – Sixth Grade and I would have 35 classmates.

Our new house in Big Sandy.

My fifth-grade teacher was Mrs. Humes, and since I did not know any classmates, I decided I would sit close to her. I selected the second row from the door, and the seat closest to her. It would turn out that all the boys sat on one side of the room, and all the girls sat on the other side. You won't believe this, but I accidentally chose the side where the boys were sitting. Everything went well the first day. We would be released by row for recess, and on the second day it was my row's day to be released first. I turned around and followed the other six boys. The only problem was that they all decided to go into the boy's bathroom. Yes, I followed them into the boy's bathroom! All of a sudden they are screaming, "There's a girl in our bathroom!" I turned around, ran so quickly and spent that recess in the furnace room, until the janitor came. It seemed a little strange to have an indoor bathroom, and to have a cafeteria where you could either eat the lunch you brought from home, or actually buy a ticket for a hot lunch.

Daddy would continue to go to the farm and do the seeding in the spring and fall. We would plant wheat and barley at both times of the year, and harvest the crops in August. He would also go out during the summer to turn the soil over, in order to get rid of the weeds. He did what was called strip farming, where every other field was planted while the other one rested, thus giving the nutrients time to come back into the soil. We always moved back out to the farm for the summer. During the 1950's we had some good crops, where the wheat would yield 35 to 45 bushels per acre. We even had a strip of barley that went for 60 bushels to the acre. We were not rich! After spending $6,000 for a new combine, good prices for crops did not go very far. By this time, we had gotten rid of all our animals, except two milk cows that we pastured at a barn on the outskirts of Big Sandy.

I also remember that I thought I would be rich if I could marry a man that was earning $25,000 a year, and we could afford to live in a house that cost $50,000. In 2017, the average salary in Seattle is $68,912 and the median household income is $80,349, while the average house price is $747,500. Oh my, how things have changed!

My first best friend, Kathleen Branagan, would love to spend the night with me, so that she could go with Daddy to milk the cows each morning. Little did I know, that those crazy cows would help me find a good friend. Kathleen came and spent a week with me at the farm during the harvest of 1957. By this time, at age 10, I could drive around the farmyard. One of my favorite things to play involved driving the car around the farmyard and stopping at each building. I was pretending that I was a housewife running errands, and that the barn was the bank, and the chicken coop was the grocery store. I remember one day, when Kathleen was staying with me; my parents had driven the car to town, and we were left with just the big wheat truck. We drove up and down different roads and all around the farmyard. All of a sudden when we are in the middle of the yard, I could not get it into gear to shift down. None of the vehicles had automatic gears at that time. We had to learn how to shift in order to change gears, and we would often grind the gears in the process. My parents came home and Daddy, who was very easy going yelled, "Why the hell is the truck in the middle of the yard?" He had been in the Army, and had learned to swear a bit! I said, "Oh, I was just trying to put it in the shade," (it was always best for us to park vehicles in the shade). He was on to me though, as he said, "The hell you were, you were out in the middle of the yard!"

In the summer, I loved wearing "pedal pushers" (known as capri pants today). I was so proud of my turquoise and white polka-dot pedal pushers. I had made them in Home Economics class and modeled them at the Variety Show. We would wear these with our "thongs" or what are known as flip flops, (thongs have a much different meaning today).

That same summer, my nine-year-old cousin, Sherry Nepil, came to stay. She lived in Havre (where I was born) but in 1960 moved to Las Vegas. She was a tomboy, and always wanted to wrestle or play jacks. I didn't like to wrestle or play jacks. She later became a policewoman, so she could wrestle plenty. She wanted to ride horses and since we did not have any horses, we went to ride some of the neighbor's horses. My cousin Sherry, and Terry Jurenka, were riding on the adult horses, and that meant that Renee Jurenka and I had to ride together on the pony. Well, the pony, did not want to get out of sight of her stablemates. Sherry and Terry couldn't care less; they just kept riding ahead, leaving us in their dust. While Renee was sitting behind me and I was in the saddle, our pony took off and tried to get rid of us. Renee was sliding off and nearly pulled me with her; when the pony decided to go right next to a tree trunk. That caused all the branches to hit us in the face. I braved the pony storm until the pony finally saw the other horses, galloped full bore to the fence, and reared on her hind legs, then landed us on the ground! Thankfully, our landing was softened by some hay and a little horse manure. I was very happy to get off that pony, (with no broken bones), I didn't even care what I landed in. It took me 40 years before I was brave enough to get on a horse again!

I was just starting to feel fairly confident by the time the sixth grade rolled around, since by then I knew most of the kids in my class.

But just to shake things up a little, my teacher in sixth grade turns out to be a male. His name was Mr. Johnson, and I liked him until he wrote in my report card, "Loretta is a good student. She is capable of doing better with some of her work." Mind you, I was getting A's and B's. I guess he thought I was meant to be a straight A student!

School Days 1957-1958

By the end of sixth grade, I thought I really had this big school down, but now it was time for a new challenge. Even though seventh and eighth grades were considered junior high, they were in the same building as the high school. So here I am again, needing to find my way around a new school, plus find a new room for each class period, and trying to remember my locker number and code. I had nightmares for years, that I could never remember what my class schedule was, or how to open my locker!

During my seventh grade, I decided I needed to earn some money. What could be so hard about babysitting, I wondered. I soon found out while babysitting for three Berlinger families, they lived just a quarter of a block away, so that seemed perfect. The husbands were musicians, and the wives were all from Ireland and loved to go dancing. They would have all the kids stay with me at the one house, I could easily be babysitting the five kids, normally not too bad, since they all went to bed. The parents would leave at about 8:00 p.m. in order to get tuned up to play. They would return about 3:00 a.m., after the dance was over, and they let me sleep when the kids were asleep. The only downfall was that they did not have a telephone. One night they left, (all was well), until the six-month old baby started crying. I tried everything from rocking to singing, but could not get her to settle down. The night wore on and by 11:00 p.m., I would be shedding my own tears, not knowing what to do to soothe her. There was no way that I could leave the kids to get my Mother. I was a zombie, with a blouse wet from tears, but finally about 1:00 a.m. the baby and I were both asleep in the rocking chair. The next time I babysat they told me that they had given her a diet pill by mistake, thinking it was a baby aspirin. Poor little baby, no wonder she was cramped up with pain.

The next time I agreed to babysit it was for a Sunday afternoon, what could go wrong at this time, I thought to myself. It was a sunny day so the two oldest kids wanted to go out and play in the yard. In the 50's it was common that kids played outside without any supervision, and were just told to come in before dark. It seems like all kids like to play with water, so the Berlinger kids turned the hose on to get a drink of water, not paying much attention to where they dropped the hose. Thank God I happened to go outside to check on them, and here the hose, had been dropped by the open basement window. I screamed when I saw it, and quickly shut it off, or else there would have been a lot more than two inches of water in the basement. I recruited the kids, and we spent the next two hours draining the water and cleaning up the mess. This babysitting job was not worth the $ .50 an hour that I was making, so I quit!

· 9 ·

HIGH SCHOOL HOPES AND DREAMS
1959-1964

By the time I started the eighth grade, I felt very comfortable in my classroom, and in Big Sandy. Let me take a moment and describe Big Sandy for you. While I lived there, the population was about 900 people, but in 2017 it had decreased to 582 people. My high school class size was 42, although there were only 37 that graduated with me. In recent years, there might only be 10 students in the high school graduating class. There are currently 70 students in high school, which consists of 9th-12th grade, and 23 students in junior high school, which consists of 7th and 8th grade. There was only one main street, and everything was on that street: the bank, the post office, a clothing store, a drug store, a dry cleaner, a bowling alley, a library, a movie theatre, two grocery stores, two restaurants, five bars, five churches, and four elevators for grains. When I was in junior high school, there was a youth club for sock hops (dances), which later closed due to lack of funding. As you can see, there wasn't a lot to keep teenagers occupied, thus, we had to create our own fun. We were 34 miles from Havre, and 72 miles from Great Falls, where the action was.

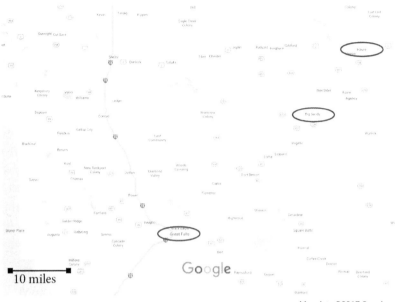

I hadn't had a boyfriend since first grade at Hopp School. It was time for me to have a boyfriend. Little did I know, that in 1960 I would even get a sneak peek at my future husband! How would that happen, when I didn't officially meet him for seven and one-half more years. I did not belong to the junior high school band, but my best friend, Kathleen Branagan, played the French Horn in band. Every year the Great Falls Hockey Club would invite a high school band to come play on Sunday afternoon. On February 28, 1960, it was designated Big Sandy Day, for the game between the Great Falls Americans and Lethbridge, Alberta (Canada) Club. Kathleen invited me to go along, and Duane Johnson was playing hockey for the Great Falls Americans. Kathleen and I were very bored, so we would run around whenever she did not have to play her French Horn. I was 13 years old, and Duane was 21 years old. He thought he was very cool with his long, slicked-back hair style. If someone had said, "You are going to marry that man someday," I would have burst out laughing. Although, likewise, if someone had said, "You are going to marry that skinny, flat-chested blonde girl someday," he would have said "No way!"

Back to my eighth-grade boyfriend, Ron Wooley, who I dated for one day! The extent of our dating was, he walked me home from school, and carried my books! The main reason I was convinced he was my boyfriend was that one day, while listening to the KMON radio station, there was a requested song at Sandy's Drive-In in Great Falls. It was for Loretta from Ron. The song was by Elvis Presley and was called, "Won't You Wear My Ring Around Your Neck". I never did know the truth, but it was my hope and dream that lasted for a year.

It was a truth that became stronger when I was selected to crown the Blessed Virgin Mary and learned to pray a special prayer. This was held at St. Margaret Mary Catholic Church. I wore a white dress, and white veil, and my sister Lorraine lead the procession of Father Ferretti and the two altar boys. It is a traditional Roman Catholic ritual that occurs in the month of May, where every year the Mother of Jesus Christ is crowned and honored. I soon memorized a Novena for Impossible Requests to Mother Mary, and she receives impossible requests from me still today!

Remember, O most gracious Virgin Mary,
that never was it known that anyone who
fled to your protection, implored your help
or sought your intercession, was ever
left unaided.

Inspired with this confidence,
I fly to you, O Virgin of virgins, my Mother.
To you I come; before you I stand, sinful
And sorrowful.

O Mother of the Word
Incarnate, despise not my petitions, but in
your mercy hear and answer me.
Amen

I was praying that I would not fall down while crowning the Blessed Virgin Mary.

When I started the 9th grade (Freshman in High School), Marj was a Senior, and it was up to her class to initiate my class. I had to wear a one-piece men's underwear with the hole in the back, worse yet, on the stage of the auditorium, I had to sing "Hang Down Your Head Tom Dooley" to the entire school! Being a part of the Church Choir, did not mean I was a good singer. You could see my red face for miles, and I nearly died of embarrassment.

My year as a ninth grader brought both dreams of love, and disappointments in love. Kathleen had been my best friend for four years. People said we were two peas in a pod. She was a cheerleader, and was riding with us to an out of town basketball game, and on the way, we started discussing that we both wanted to date Dennis Johnson. He was a tall, good looking classmate that had never dated anyone. I happened to say that I had "an in," since Carol Anne was dating Dennis' older brother Clark. Dennis was on the Varsity Basketball Team, a natural basketball player at 6'1". During the Junior Varsity game he happened to sit behind me, and of course I was flirting with him, while Kathleen was in the front row with the rest of the cheerleaders. On the way home Kathleen was extremely quiet, and I could tell she was mad, meanwhile I was very happy. Soon Dennis asked me out, and we had a great time double dating with Mike and Carol, Steve and Lynn (later Steve and Vicki,) and Glen and Penny. He also asked me to the Prom, which was held on April 22, 1961.

Carol, myself, and Jerri Ann with our dates Mike, Dennis, and David are all dressed for the prom.

We had dance cards that we used to trade dances with other couples, but you always saved the first and last dance for your date. Of course, I saved five dances for us, but did trade one dance with Kathleen and her date Robbie.

The theme of the prom was "Stars Fell on Alabama."

The relationship between Kathleen and I had dissipated so badly that we would cross the street, rather than run into each other. The boys in our class were quite mean to her. At the swimming pool they would dunk her, and hold her down for quite some time. Meanwhile, she had become friends with a 10th grade girl who went to the Lutheran Youth Group, where Dennis attended. Her new friend was constantly telling Dennis that he needed to break up with me, and date Kathleen.

Meanwhile, Dennis and I dated for eight months. One night, he said, "I love you!" I was so shocked that I responded, "Oh, you don't really know what you are saying!" That was probably not the best response, but I thought we were too young to get serious. In October, he told me that he needed to take a break for a while to figure things out. I knew instantly what that meant, and sure enough, he started dating Kathleen within two weeks. It took three years before we rekindled our friendship, and it was never quite the same. She would later say that Dennis and I were a much better couple than Dennis and she were.

Dianne Humphrey would become my best friend for the remaining high school years. She and I had a love of adventure in common, and we had a lot of fun laughing. She asked Nancy Reichelt and I to be her attendants when she was a Carnival Queen Candidate in 1962.

Dianne's attendants getting ready for the Grand March.

I went on to date numerous other boys but none very seriously. I went to the Prom in 1962 and 1963 with Jim Stevens, but never considered him my boyfriend. My date for the Senior Prom was Terry Dixon, who was honored to be crowned Prom King.

Jim and I are dressed for the Prom in 1962. Mom bought my light blue dress in Great Falls for $19.98.

Jim and I are ready to go to the prom in 1963. This was a hand-me-down dress from Marj.

One date turned out to be very embarrassing. My parents always required that we had a curfew, except on graduation night. They said I could stay out all night, and not have a curfew! After the ceremony, and a graduation party at the Hammonds' house, Kathleen, Dan Beaudette, Mike Hammond and I left in Dan's car. Well, no one mentioned that Mike had a curfew, and here comes Mr. Hammond (his Dad and the school Principal) looking for us. He found us driving around on the country highway. Granted, it was 6:30 a.m., Mike and I were in the back seat, and I was sitting next to him while he had his arm around me, (it was all quite innocent). Needless to say, we took Mike home immediately and I went home after that. My parents were just getting up for breakfast but they were surprised to see me even then.

As a Senior, I was nominated as a candidate for Carnival Queen and Dean Robertson was the candidate for Carnival King. Our posters would say, "FOR A TEAM THAT'S KEEN VOTE LORETTA AND DEAN".

Dean and I are ready for the Grand March.
They discontinued the idea of having attendants.

I was elected and installed as the Treasurer of FHA (Future Homemakers of America). On May 17, 1963, I gave the devotion at the FHA Variety Show. There were eight purposes of the FHA group, number one was "to promote a growing appreciation of the joys and satisfactions of homemaking!" You would never see that in today's society! I was also elected Vice President of the Senior Class, it was a nice position as the job required very little work. I would also be part of the Senior Class Play, (although we would never have a formal Drama Club or training). I took Typing and Shorthand Classes, and won awards in each, typing 60 words per minute. I thought that typing would help if I wanted to be a secretary, not realizing it would be a necessary skill for using a laptop or a smart phone today.

Dianne Humphrey went on to be the Valedictorian of the graduating class, and Kathleen Branagan was the Salutatorian. I had smart friends!

One of my most upsetting days, in high school, was the day that Carol Anne had cut my hair so short that I looked like one of the boys. I think she was mad at me because I had tattled about her, and she really took the scissors after me. I stayed home from school, brushing my hair all day for three days, in hopes that it would grow. No luck though, and I had to get back to my studies. I walked in and Mr. Green, (who was quite humorous when it came to other things) said, "What happened to you over the weekend Loretta? Did you run into a lawn mower?" By this time, the entire class was staring and laughing at me. Carol Anne had started as a bookkeeper at the Beauty Salon but somehow, we assumed she was a hair stylist. When she had scissors in her hand, I never came near her again.

One day, in Mr. Green's English Literature class, we were studying Shakespeare, and were to memorize Romeo and Juliet, then present in front of the class. During the part where you would say, "My heart is in the coffin," I kept getting it into my head to say, "My head is in the coffin." Sure enough, when I got up to present to the class, I said, "My head is in the coffin," and the whole class started roaring with laughter, then I started laughing so hard I couldn't even talk. I would try to resume talking, but could not stop laughing. Finally, Mr. Green said, "Loretta, go sit down. I think your head IS in the coffin!"

I would also have some embarrassing moments with Mr. Hammond during geometry class. His nickname was Swede Hammond, and he said I was like the Swedes because I always used my hands to talk. He would love to make me go to the board to prove my hypothesis, so that he could have a good laugh. Between talking with my hands, and trying to use the protractor without the chalk squeaking, I was a real comedian. I didn't understand half of the problems, but was fortunate when Dennis Johnson would help me with my homework. It was great that I could turn in a completed assignment, but I was in real trouble if I had to go up and explain it to the class.

There were times when classmates were not very kind to the teachers. One time, a teacher in study hall was scratching his crotch, and a classmate would say, "Are you digging for gold?" We also had a teacher who was a "yeller and a tyrant." His pants were unzipped one day when a classmate told him the same thing. He just stood behind the chair and refused to lean over and zip them up. I thought this was a little stubborn on his part.

Most of our activities happened around sports and school activities. I was on the starting five of the girls' basketball team. It was only intramural, so we were not allowed to travel very far. My favorite sports were basketball, swimming, and dancing. The highlight of my high school years happened in 1963, when our school won the Montana Class B Boys State Basketball Championship.

Back row from left: Bill Conquergood, Stan Klimas, Sonny Broesder, Bob Lanning, Roger Jappe. Middle row from left: Gary Robertson, Ricky Richter, Dennis Johnson, Ronnie Wooley. Front row from left: Glen Kulbeck, Mike Hammond.

Player	Light	Dark	Position	Height	Yr.
STAN KLIMAS	42	11	F-C	6— 3	Sr.
SONNY BROESDER	32	33	F-C	6— 4	Sr.
BOB LANNING	34	55	F	6— 2	Sr.
GARY ROBERTSON	20	12	G	5—10	Sr.
RICKY RICHTER	30	3	G	5—11	Sr.
BILL CONQUERGOOD	30	4	F	6— 1	Sr.
MIKE HAMMOND	10	15	G	5— 8	Jr.
DENNIS JOHNSON	44	44	F-C	6— 0	Jr.
ROGER JAPPE	14	14	F	6— 0	Soph.
MAURICE JOHNSON	22	22	F	5—11	Soph.
GLEN KULBECK	12	13	G	5— 7	Jr.
RON WOOLEY	24	5	F	5— 9	Jr.

Coach—H. W. "Swede" Hammond
Assistant Coach—Ed Ellingson
Student Managers—Dana Dixon, James Sohm
Student Trainer—David Hashley
Cheerleaders—Suzanne Madison, Carol Larson, Carol Grubb, Kathleen Branagan, Penny Courtnage
School Colors—Purple and Gold
School Song—"Rouser" (University of Minnesota)

WELCOME TO HAVRE . . .

Teams and Fans

FAIR HOTEL

For Comfort and Convenience

We won the District Tournament and the Divisional Tournament before winning the State Tournament.

Marj had started working at the Big Sandy Drugstore, so I did too. We would start out making $ .65 an hour and when she was a Senior she was making $ .90 an hour. I started on July 9, 1961 when I was 14 ½ years old. In 1967, Lorraine followed me, and worked at the drugstore. It was a wonderful job, and entailed mostly waiting on customers, ordering merchandise, and stocking the shelves. The job also included stocking the magazines, tearing the cover off the old one that did not sell, and returning it for credit. That left a lot of magazines (without front covers) to take home and read. The drugstore had a cashew machine with warm salted cashews, a delicious snack after school! The worst part was when there were no customers, or special projects, and you had to dust the merchandise. I was very bored with that. Once, it was very upsetting seeing a man pass out in the store, trying to be discreet I yelled for the pharmacist. The pharmacist revived him with smelling salts, while I stood trembling in the corner. In summer and on Saturdays they would like you to wear a white uniform dress, similar to the white jacket that the pharmacist wore. We didn't have to wear the uniform when we worked after school.

I am standing by the pharmacy in my white uniform.

I am standing in the card section.

Once I started working, I did not go out to the farm during harvest. I would stay with Doris and Cliff, who lived in town and were neighbors and friends. They were a young couple with three young kids, thus, I had a lot of fun with them. In 1962 Doris and Cliff took me on a wonderful trip to Seattle for the Worlds' Fair, also known as the Century 21 Exposition, little did I know that I would live in Seattle one day. In Seattle I visited Carol Anne, who was living on Capitol Hill and attending Beauty School from where she graduated. For a flat-lander, walking Seattle's steep hills was a huge chore. She and I went out, had pie and cokes, only to discover Carol Anne was flat broke. Thankfully I had a few meager pennies and paid for us!

I would often babysit or help with chores for Doris and Cliff (I am embarrassed to recall this memory). As I would try to get their pudgy little boy to eat his baby food, we would play this game and I would call him "fat boy", then he would giggle and open his mouth to eat. I later learned that when he was four years old, and at the local barbershop, he called the current school principal, "Fat Boy." Lesson learned, your words matter.

Thankfully, Daddy had been working steadily as a builder since we had moved to Big Sandy; we had been hailed out at the farm for three years in a row in the early 1960's. It was always a frightening experience to see the black clouds gather, accompanied by thunder and lightning. We worried that the hail would be next, and overnight incomes for the whole year disappear. My parents would take out hail insurance, but that usually only covered the seed for the next year's crop.

During my high school years, there were several national events that caused tremendous change in the United States. On May 25, 1961, President Kennedy announced that we would put a man on the moon. Sadly, he did not live to see that, as he was assassinated on November 22, 1963. This put the entire country into mourning. To this day, no President has been so dearly loved. You would always remember where you were that day. I had left school for home, and was getting ready to go to a dental appointment in Havre.

An enjoyable highlight on February 9, 1964 was watching The Beatles perform on The Ed Sullivan Show. About two-fifths of the total American population (73 million) watched (most were screaming) that evening. They were popular for decades. Finally, on July 20, 1969 we landed the first humans on the moon.

· 10 ·

A TEENAGER'S ADVENTURES
1960-1964

I was born with an adventurous spirit, and that was soon enhanced when I became a teenager. I often would be in trouble with Mom and that would mean I was grounded. Daddy (my older sisters and I called him Daddy until his death), was very easy-going and did very little of the disciplining. He was also quite quiet and so it was a challenge to engage him in a conversation. He loved baseball, and I realized that was the way that we could bond with each other. I learned all the names of the players on his favorite baseball team, the Milwaukee Braves (who would later become the Atlanta Braves), doing this made a difference in the quality of the relationship we shared.

I always liked to sleep until the last second, jumping out of bed and throwing my clothes on, I would head out the door after a quick breakfast. It would infuriate Mom that I never had time to make my bed or hang up my clothes. One time, she got so mad that she took all my clothes out of the closet and threw them all over the bed and the floor. She said, "There you go, they are never hung up anyway."

Boy, I was furious at her, but knew that she wouldn't speak to me for several days. A very hard worker, in hot summer she didn't think anything of waking us up at 6:00 a.m., so we could help weed the garden. In the house, we had to help scrub the walls down, or clean the cupboards, she would say, "Well, you can take a nap this afternoon." Whoever wanted to take a nap when you were a teenager and the pool was open.

September of 1961 was a tough time for Mom, as Marj left for college and Darell started first grade. It would be the first time that none of her children would be at home with her and she felt very lonesome. How would I know this? She kept a diary for 50 years, and most diaries did not have a lock. It was my "secret weapon" in knowing if she was mad at me for something.

I liked to "sneak" things, or do things that I hoped no one, (particularly my parents) would ever find out. We were never allowed to see a "B" rated movie. Today, almost every movie would be rated B! We were only allowed to see PG rated movies. When I was dating Dennis, we went to see the B rated movie "Hell to Eternity". It was a true story about a young man who was horrified at the carnage of World War II. He disobeyed orders and went behind enemy lines, talking the Japanese into willful surrender, saving thousands of lives on both sides. Although, they never found out that I went to this movie, it didn't seem like such a bad movie to me!

I was not so lucky on another occasion when I "snuck" out. It was one of those nights that I was grounded and I was supposed to be babysitting. I was already in my shorty pajamas when my cousin, Jerri Ann, showed up with two boys and wanted me to go to the dance. She said, "Just put your coat and heels on, and no one will notice that you are in your pajamas". I had this long black coat with a fur collar, it had one problem, it was a swing coat with only one hook at the top. Right away, one of the boys who was a really good dancer asked me to dance, needless to say, my coat was swinging open showing a lot of my leg. After a few dances, I said, "I've got to get home, my parents are playing cards and they don't stay out that late." Right when I was ready to get into the car, my parents drove by slowly, staring at me! I knew I would be busted but didn't expect Daddy to be so mad. He would never raise a hand (yes, in that day my parents believed in spanking), but as soon as I walked in the door, he slapped me and I flew across our large kitchen. Darn it, I was grounded for longer!

I always liked driving the car or pickup around, especially after we drove on the farm at such a young age. It didn't matter to me if I didn't have my driver's license. One Sunday afternoon while my parents were gone, Kathleen was over visiting me. We were soon bored, and decided that we needed to go "cruise the drag." This was when we would drive up and down Main Street, and honk at each other, or pull over to talk. Mr. Hammond was driving by, and he got a big smile on his face. The next day he proceeded to tell the whole class and call me "Barney Oldfield," after a famous auto racing driver that set many speed records. Thankfully, my parents never heard this, thus it was my secret. That same Sunday afternoon, we decided we better get home and get the pickup back in the garage. It wasn't so bad backing out, but became very difficult to drive in to the garage. I first tried driving in and found that it would start to scrape the passenger door, Kathleen said, "Let me try", well, she made it worse. By this time the pickup was stuck, scraped wood off the side of the garage, and put a big scratch all along the side of the door. We got out and screamed at each other, "What are we going to do now?" We noticed that this boy who was always trying to date us was visiting at his grandparent's house just on the other side of the street. I yelled, "James, could you please come help us?" He came racing across the street and soon was able to get the pickup in the garage. I said, "Okay, thanks, that is all we need." It wasn't really all we needed, since we still had to fix the door. Rummaging through Daddy's tools I found some sanding paper, we soon got the wood smoothed down but now needed white paint. I desperately searched all through the garage but could not find any; unwilling to give up I had a bright idea that we could use white shoe polish. We always kept white shoe polish because we had to polish our white saddle shoes, and even our white tennis shoes. Amazingly, the white shoe polish solved that problem, but we still had the big scratch on the pickup. The next day, Daddy said to Carol Anne, "How did you get that big scratch on the side of the pickup?" She said, "That wasn't me." They looked at me and I said, "How could it be me, I don't even have a license!" Carol Anne got stuck with the blame. After cutting my hair so short, I was finally even!

Another driving adventure came one night when Dianne and I became bored with driving around Big Sandy. By this time, I had my driver's license, Marj was attending college in Havre, and I no longer had to babysit my sister and brother, since Lorraine was 10 years of age. Mom and Daddy were at a country dance, and we were driving around in Daddy's blue and white pickup truck. Mind you, I had already masterly maneuvered getting the pickup out of the garage, and mega-masterly without hitting Robertson's car which was parked right behind it. There was snow on the ground so I had to drag my foot along the tire track to cover any tracks and hide the evidence. We had one problem though, it was nearing 11:00 p.m., all the gas stations were closed, and the pickup gas tank was approaching empty. No fear, Dianne's Dad had a gas pump at their house, so secretly she filled the gas tank, and we were on our way to Havre. We were headed to buy a hamburger and have some fun, but before we had time to buy the hamburger, a car full of teenagers started honking and yelling at us. I got a glimpse of them and screamed to Dianne, "That's Marj, trying to catch us!" I gunned the motor and we escaped into the night. The next weekend, Marj was home from college, she said to my Mother, "I could have sworn that I saw Loretta driving Daddy's pickup last Saturday night in Havre." I said, "How could that have been me, when Robertson's car was parked in the driveway, and if you recall, Daddy said, the pickup was out of gas." They both looked at me skeptically, but were hard pressed to refute it. Whew, that was close!

One summer night I was riding around town with friends, my parents were at the farm, and everyone on Main Street stopped and wondered where we could go for a party. Most people knew that my parents were harvesting and our house would be available, together they yelled, "Let's go to Loretta's house!" I didn't want to dampen the excitement so I agreed, and soon they all pulled up. It was very difficult to keep 15 people from waking up the neighbors, we laughed into the night.

Steven Roth and I are in a tickling match.

The following Monday, Daddy would be giving me a ride to work. He calmly said, "What about this party you had Saturday night?" I quickly said, "What party?" He responded in a tone louder, "Don't what party me! I was told by Gail and Fay Morris (who lived across the street)." Then after a short pause he said, "Just don't let your Mother find out!" I sighed a huge sigh of relief and said, "Oh, I won't do that." I will be grateful for that moment the rest of my life, and I never had another party as a teenager.

Lorraine, Darell and I are standing on the front lawn with the Morris family house behind us.

In March of my Senior year, Kathleen and I were both being good Catholic girls and attending Mass every day during Lent. Sharon Broesder, Kathleen and I were all participating in the Senior Play. After play practice, we decided to spend the night at Sharon's house, so we could practice our lines. Since no one was home at Sharon's house, we were home alone. Kathleen and I got up and attended 7:00 a.m. Mass, then skipped school and kept working on our lines at Sharon's house until noon. Sharon wrote out three excuses, so we thought we were all set. One minor detail, Mr. Chvilicek, class sponsor and teacher, was also attending Mass. That afternoon when he was in the office he noticed we had all been absent, and the handwriting matched on all three excuses! We were busted. Because we were all leaders of the school (Sharon was Senior Class President, I was Vice- President and Kathleen was a Cheerleader), they decided to make a real example of us. We were tagged the Truancy Triplets, and had to stay after school for a week. Interestingly enough, my parents were not that upset, and I didn't even get grounded!

Graduation was May 20, 1964, and I was blessed to receive many wonderful presents. The best present I received was a vacation by train to Chicago and on to a cabin on Lake Michigan, owned by my friend Stefanie's family. Stefanie Hetzel, (whom I had met at Vacation Bible School) and I were both teaching Bible studies to the Native American children. The Rocky Boy Reservation, a 35-minute drive from Big Sandy, was home for the Chippewa Cree Tribe. While in Chicago, I visited my cousin, Mary Ann Nepil, and my namesake's family, Loretta Gliege. Mary Ann was an only child and lead a very sheltered life, I thought it strange that she had never been to a post office to mail a letter, or pick up a package. Although, I thought I was quite knowledgeable after running a farm house, I found out on the train ride to be sorely mistaken. My assigned seat was with a portly woman who spread her arm over into my seat, annoyed, I made my way to the Dome Car. Quite soon, a good-looking guy came and sat by me, he reached in his pocket and offered me a cigarette. I replied, "No thanks, I don't smoke." He asked if I minded if he smoked. I quickly responded, "No, I don't mind." After thinking about it, I decided that I should act grownup and have a cigarette. I coughed a few times as I inhaled, so soon decided I would fake it and not inhale. When I was finished, I dropped the cigarette butt into the ashtray between us, to my horror here comes all this smoke from our ashtray. I had failed to press the butt against the side and put it out. So embarrassed, I promptly ran back to my seat by the portly woman. When nightfall came, she started to snore, so that really drove me back to the Dome Car. My friend was still there, so we visited for a while, and then started to go to sleep. When I woke up, he had his arm around me and had started to put the move on me. It was okay when he kissed me, but when his hands were on my breast, I said, "You need to stop right now!" I quickly got up, and ran to my assigned seat, where I remained for the rest of the trip.

· 11 ·

OUR FADING FARM LIFE
1964-1987

1 964 was a year of many changes for our family, Carol Anne and Marj both got married and I left for college. Carol Anne and Vern Nelson got married June 6, 1964, and I was a bridesmaid. She got strep throat and a high fever the day before the wedding, so Marj threatened to step in and marry Vern if she wasn't well. That didn't go over very well, since Marj and Vern had dated for a short time. Carol Anne and Vern's honeymoon did not go smoothly either, as they were struck by the Great Flood of June 1964 while attempting to go to Waterton, Canada, only to be the last car to cross a bridge before it collapsed. Eventually they had to turn back, when the river had poured over the highway at Cardston, Canada. This was the worst flood in the state history of Montana, where it claimed 31 lives.

Marj married David O'Reilly on December 28, 1964, and again, I was a bridesmaid. It was another eventful weather experience for the year, as Big Sandy had recorded a record amount of snow. My parents hired the Chouteau County snowplow to clear our driveway and street; (typically we would just shovel the driveway). The wedding guests living in the country had to travel in their large wheat trucks, due to the difficult roads, fortunately, we had hired horses and a sleigh for the bride and groom. Our family continued to have a strong bond, and we enjoyed getting together as much as possible.

Our family has our photo done professionally in 1965. Standing left to right is Marj, Loretta, Carol Anne, and Lorraine. Mom, Darell, and Daddy are seated.

My Senior Year in College.

Farming continued to have highs and lows, which caused stress and worry. Daddy had started to feel the strain of driving back and forth to the farm, especially when Mom could not join him during Lorraine and Darell's school year. On June 30, 1965, a major hail storm hit, destroying many crops on our farm and neighbors' farms. It was accompanied by intense rain, flooding our basement and root cellar. In turn, 1966 was a year of bumper crops! The wheat yielded a record 42 bushels to the acre in one area, and an average in others of 25–30 bushels to the acre. Barley was higher at 30 – 45 bushels to the acre.

What a surprise, not one of us five children were told that Mom and Daddy sold the farm to a local farmer on August 30, 1967. The two son-in-laws, were very disappointed, as they had enjoyed helping Daddy on the farm, and wished they could have purchased it. The new owner and his family only farmed the land, never moving into our house, choosing instead to remain living in their house. Sadly, after 18 years of the ups and downs of farming, the purchaser lost the farm. The bank took it over when the new owner defaulted, and could not meet his financial commitments. Sadly, our family farm life faded more.

• *EPILOGUE* •

1987-2017

Twenty years later on June 22, 1987, our family members and spouses returned to the farm, to see the farm house one last time. We wore matching t-shirts with the slogan created by Kerry O'Reilly, (Marj's son), "MEMORIES ARE THE CHARM, WHEN WE COME BACK TO LADDIE'S FARM". It was sad to see the vandalism inside the house, everything was damaged, including sinks broken in the kitchen and bathroom. No one had lived in the house, thus allowing thieves to break in. Aside from the interior of the house, everything looked the same, except the road had been converted to fields.

84

The granary and shed for the combine.

The farmhouse, garage, and Grandpa's apartment. The road to the farm had been plowed over and turned into a field.

The family poses while their hair blew in the wind. From left to right – back row: Loretta and Marj; center row: Carol Anne, Mom, and Daddy; front row: Lorraine and Darell

I am going to pick the eggs!

Our walk down memory lane also took us to visit Hopp School, Osterman's Grove, and several neighbors. Hopp School had also been the victim of vandalism, with the letters HOPP stolen.

The paint has faded from a memorable schoolhouse.

I am so grateful we all went back to see the farm. It saddens me to have to end this chapter with the news that shortly after our visit, the second owners of our farm (who bought it from the bank), burnt the house to the ground and removed any buildings in the way, to free the land for farming. The three steel granaries and a large shed for the combine were the only ones of value remaining, little else. Farmers had been forced to buy more land in order to be profitable. The only thing of value was the 1,000 acres ready for crops.

On February 5, 1968 Grandpa Nepil passed away at 82 from a heart attack. He was my last living grandparent, the end of a generation. My most painful memory was February 10, 1998, when Daddy died of cancer at the age of 80. He had survived lung cancer surgery, a quadruple bi-pass and a stroke; I believed he had nine lives and would never leave us. We buried him on February 14, Valentine's Day with utmost love and respect for a wonderful husband, dad, father-in-law and grandfather. He died prior to meeting my three wonderful grandchildren. I wish he could have seen Gabriel as an usher at church, since that was his job for many years. It would have been amazing if he could have seen Beatrice, our actress, perform in commercials and on several television series. It would have been fun for him to see Chloe using her carpenter skills, as she makes a shelf with her boards, hammer, and nails. I said, "You are quite the carpenter girl," and she replied, "Thanks, I take that as a compliment."

Dear Reader,
I am honored that you allowed me
to share my past, who I am, and what
legacy I leave for you. This book has
allowed me to look at my memories, both
joyous and painful ones. These written
memories were what I believed to be
most meaningful, and the process made
me realize how many beliefs gave meaning
to my life.

Loretta Johnson

ADDITIONAL FAMILY PHOTOS

Helen Sevcik — Fall-1941

Helen Sevcik is all dressed up in her hat and heels.

nepils. Jan 17, / 9 4 2

Laddie, Helen, and Grandma Nepil pose on January 17, 1942, after the wedding.

Laddie is in his uniform in Kentucky, in June of 1942.

Grandma Sevcik and Helen Nepil - Mother & Daughter in 1942.

Combining 1946 - Ladd, Eddie & Bill.

Laddie is combining in 1946.

From left to right: Marj, Daddy is holding me while I squint from the sun, Mommy is holding Carol Anne.

Grandpa and Grandma Nepil and Loretta Gliege joined us for a picture. Grandma, in her apron, must be cooking.

Daddy is hanging on to me tightly so I don't blow away. Notice Marj and Carol Anne's saddle shoes.

Marj, Carol Anne, Gerald Rutledge and I are playing games on the floor.

Carol Anne and I are all dressed in our long white stockings.

Mommy, Daddy and I brace against the Montana wind.

We don't look very happy but I think the sun is in our eyes! Notice the big dirt hill in the back of the house. I drove my tricycle down it once (only once)!

Aunt Marie with cousin Mary Ann, Aunt Ann with cousins Jerri Ann, Glen & Blanche, Grandma Nepil with us 3 are enjoying a family reunion.

Standing in front of church with Father Beltussen and Grandpa Sevcik. We all needed to wear hats to church.

In 1955, the family is all dressed for Easter Sunday.

Christmas of 1955, we spent with our cousins, Bonnie and Tim Sevcik.

Grandma and Grandpa Nepil at their Great Falls home at 3516 2nd Avenue.

Grandma Nepil with her grandkids. I am the third from left. Judy, Allen, and Larry Cline, Jerri Ann and Blanche Nepil, Lee Nepil, and the three of us are enjoying a fun family get together.

Four generations: Beatrice, Lorraine, me, and Mom. My Mother uses a walker after several falls.

I love being a grandmother to Gabriel, Beatrice and Chloe. It has been so fun to travel to Hong Kong for a ride on a rickshaw, go trick or treating as a witch in Vancouver BC, ride the Carousel at Christmas in Seattle, and tell farm stories while having a slumber party!

ACKNOWLEDGMENTS

My heartfelt gratitude to my parents, Laddie and Helen Nepil, who raised us in a loving, caring, faith-based home, and taught us to love your family, work hard, support your neighbors, and appreciate the fruits of the earth. Mom, your 50 years of diaries, were invaluable in helping me with the sequence and consistency of my memories. I am so thankful for these diaries, photos, and the histories of my grandparents.

My love and thanks to my four siblings, (Marj, Carol Anne, Lorraine, and Darell) for the fun, laughter and common bond that we have shared through the whole of my life, until this very day.

To Duane Johnson, my loving husband of nearly 50 years, who has encouraged and supported me during my various careers, while always giving me my space and independence. I thank God for every day of this adventurous journey. Thank you also for your support with the writing of this book, for the numerous times you read my drafts, and gave me valuable feedback. But most of all, I thank you for creating with me, our beautiful daughters, Lorraine Marie and Denise Michelle.

Lorraine and Denise, I am forever grateful for your love, friendship, and support. Lorraine and Rob Kitsos have blessed me with the joy of my life, two beautiful and smart grandchildren, Gabriel and Beatrice. Denise and Cyrus Khambatta, what a cherished blessing it has been for you to share Chloe with me. Thank you, Gabriel, Beatrice, and Chloe; this book wouldn't exist if you hadn't encouraged me to keep telling you, more and more, Farm Stories.

Denice McLaughlin and Denise Johnson, I appreciate the edits and encouragement, as I probably would have given up a long time ago. Also, thank you to Tori Thompson Day, whose magic created the layout and book cover. Your talent is amazing.

I appreciate that in my career as Senior Architect & Design Market Manager at Teknion, an emphasis was placed on Sustainability. The acumen and strength I was able to bring to the table, were directly linked to my ancestry. Everything I knew about my grandparents and great-grandparents and saw and learned about how tenacious they were to sustain a 1000-acre farm on the Montana prairie gave me valuable insight into the importance of sustainability and how we lived while on my farm. I became a LEED AP (Leadership in Energy and Environmental Design Accredited Professional) and worked with the furniture team (which provided Red-List free materials) on the greenest commercial building in the world, where the building occupants harvested rainwater, used solar panels for their energy, and built a composting toilet system. Many of these same standards were present in my farm life from 1947–1957.

ABOUT THE AUTHOR

Loretta (Nepil) Johnson graduated from
Montana State University with a BA
degree in History. She received her 5th
Year Certification in Secondary Education.
She spent 34 years of her career in the
Interior Design industry. Loretta spent
over 30 years publishing articles and
creating proposal responses.
FARM STORIES |A Fading Dream is her
debut book. Her second book will preview
in 2018 and will be based on 50-year old
love letters, written by her boyfriend (now
husband) when he was invited to attend an
all-black university in Atlanta, Georgia.
As a white man, he broke many barriers,
while he graduated from a two-year
master's program in one year. Loretta
currently lives in Normandy Park,
Washington, a suburb of Seattle with
her husband, Duane.